FASHION FOR
WEDDINGS

FASHION FOR
WEDDINGS

images
Publishing

First published in Australia in 1999 by
The Images Publishing Group Pty Ltd
ACN 059 734 431
6 Bastow Place, Mulgrave, Victoria, 3170
Australia
Telephone: +(61 3) 9561 5544
Facsimile: +(61 3) 9561 4860
E-mail: books@images.com.au

Fashion for Weddings 2

ISBN: 1 86470 043 2

Designed by The Graphic Image Studio Pty Ltd
Mulgrave, Australia
Printed in Singapore

CONTENTS

WEDDING DRESSES

Angelina Baccini
Armadale, Victoria, Australia

Above: Knitted bodice and sleeve with Thai silk draped skirt with bow detail

Opposite Page: Hand-made knitted bodice with silk skirt with multiple box side pleats

Photo credit: courtesy Angelina Baccini

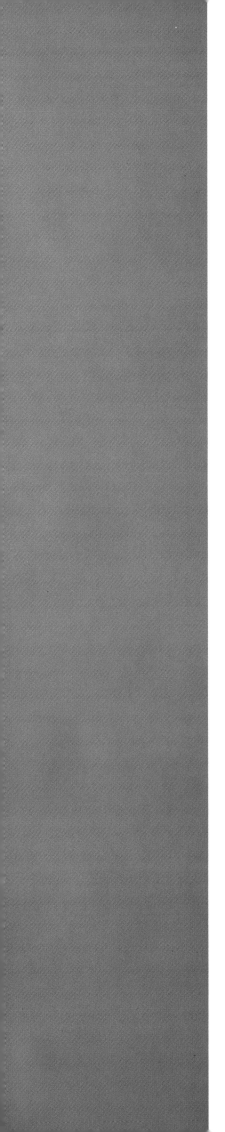

Angelina Baccini
Armadale, Victoria, Australia

Opposite Page: Hand-made floral lace bodice with silk pleated and bustled skirt

Above: Pale gold silk gown with drape under bust and gold chantilly lace detail

Photo credit: courtesy Angelina Baccini

Angelina Baccini
Armadale, Victoria, Australia

Above:

Velvet embossed bodice with mohair knit detail
and draped asymmetrical skirt

Opposite Page:

Oyster silk satin gown with hand-painted
and embroidered damask detail

Photo credit: courtesy Angelina Baccini

Angelina Baccini
Armadale, Victoria, Australia

Above: Hand-beaded crystals scattered at hemline and shoe

Opposite Page: Two-tone silk gown with hand-made knitted, striped bodice

Photo credit: courtesy Angelina Baccini

Opposite and Above:

Betrothed
Norwood, South Australia, Australia

Gowns by Betrothed

Photo credit: John Venus

Betrothed
Norwood, South Australia, Australia

Gowns by Betrothed

Photo credit: John Venus

Above and Opposite:

Betrothed
Norwood, South Australia, Australia

Gowns by Betrothed

Photo credit: John Venus

Carmi Couture Collection
New York, New York, USA

Opposite Page: Sweetheart neckline and plunging V-back princess gown of Italian satin and delicately beaded alencon lace with chapel train

Above: Flowers, bow and streamers at back waist accent a chapel train on this silk satin off-the-shoulder gown with portait collar

Photo credit: Adrian Buckmaster

Carmi Couture Collection
New York, New York, USA

Above: Silk satin sleeveless tank dress with scooped neckline features full-pleated skirt and panels of embroidery and pleated organza

Opposite Left: Silk twill gown, two-dimensional floral guipure lace with pearl trim on front and back neckline; off-the-shoulder cap sleeve, built-in petticoat, basque waist line and full centre panel pleated skirt

Opposite Right: Silk shantung A-line gown with scooped neckline, floral beaded shoulder straps enhanced with seed pearls and draped apron effect flowing into chapel train

Photo credit: Adrian Buckmaster

Carmi Couture Collection
New York, New York, USA

Opposite Page: Fit and flair A-line gown of floral patterned guipure lace and silk shantung with wide banded hem and sweep train

Above: Silk shantung gown with basque waistline, off-the-shoulder sleeves and mini boxpleats forming a full skirt flowing into a chapel train

Photo credit: Adrian Buckmaster

Connie Simonetti
Armadale, Victoria, Australia

Above:

Ivory pure silk and organza gown featuring pleating and embroidered bodice

Photo credit: Sylvanna Spagnuolo

Connie Simonetti
Armadale, Victoria, Australia

Above: Magnolia-coloured pure silk satin and French calais lace gown with draped skirt

Photo credit: Sylvanna Spagnuolo

Connie Simonetti
Armadale, Victoria, Australia

Opposite Page: Silk velvet strapless gown with hand-embroidery and draped skirt

Above: Blush-pink silk gown with hand ribbon embroidery through bodice; elaborate pleating at centre back of skirt

Photo credit: Sylvanna Spagnuolo

Connie Simonetti
Armadale, Victoria, Australia

Above:

Chardonnay-coloured pure silk gown featuring intricate embroidery

Photo credit: Sylvanna Spagnuolo

Connie Simonetti
Armadale, Victoria, Australia

Above: Strapless gown of French embroidered tulle and duchess satin; skirt and bodice feature draping

Photo credit: Sylvanna Spagnuolo

Afective Formal & Bridal Wear
East Preston, Victoria, Australia

Above:

Medieval inspired wedding gown in soft georgette
and crepe

Photo credit: Rob Stambulic

Above:

Afective Formal & Bridal Wear
East Preston, Victoria, Australia

English inspired ivory gown with rich gold
brocade inserts

Photo credit: Rob Stambulic

Marisa
New York, New York, USA

Above: Detail of alencon lace

Opposite Page: Silk satin organza Emma style A-line with alencon lace

Photo credit: Tamara Kristen for Marisa

Marisa
New York, New York, USA

Opposite Page: Model on left: Beaded Venise tank silk shantung gown
Model on right: Traditional on-shoulder beaded Venise silk shantung gown

Above Left: Detail of self beading

Above Right: Model on left: Silk satin organza gown with beaded straps and waist
Model on right: Silk shantung gown with elongated torso and self beading

Photo credit: Tamara Kristen for Marisa

Marisa
New York, New York, USA

Above: Detail silk satin beaded alencon

Opposite Page: Model on left: Silk satin Emma A-line gown
                    Model on right: Silk satin beaded alencon tank style gown

Photo credit: Tamara Kristen for Marisa

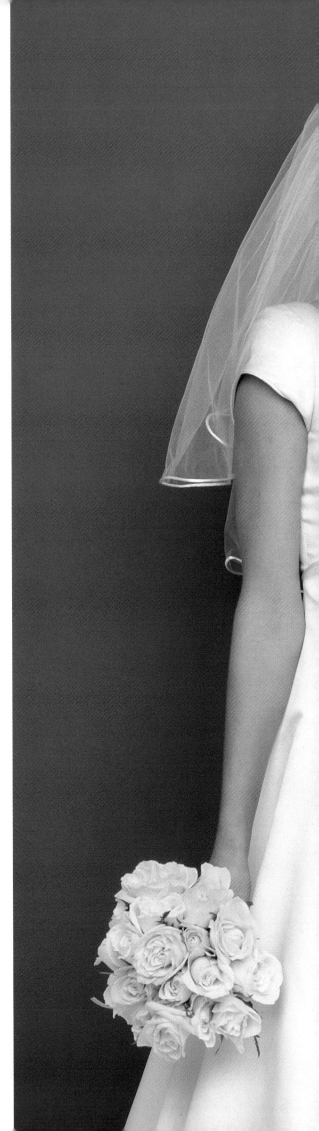

Mika Inatome
New York City, New York, USA

Opposite Page: Silk satin crepe criss-cross back with detachable train

Above: French silk satin stretch with ruched
collar and sleeves

Photo credit: courtesy Mika Inatome

Mika Inatome
New York City, New York, USA

Above: Double silk-crepe, silk chiffon and pearl beaded
                 appliques

Opposite Page: Heavily beaded, silk chiffon tunic gown with side slits

Photo credit: courtesy Mika Inatome

Peter Langner
Rome, Italy

Chiara: bias cut silk Mikado A-line gown featuring horizontal seaming with sash bow tails in back and boat neckline

Photo credit: Omar Keiroui

Peter Langner
Rome, Italy

Opposite Page: Stella: bias cut silk crepe gown featuring boat neckline, deep back décolleté and draped shoulder panel forming train

Above: Susanna: bias cut white silk Mikado gown, asymmetric cut with bow details and draping

Photo credit: courtesy Peter Langner

Peter Langner
Rome, Italy

Above:
Perla: silk organza gown with bow detail on shoulder

Photo credit: courtesy Peter Langner

Peter Langner
Rome, Italy

Above: Celia: silk Mikado A-line gown with bustier and sash bow in back,
illusion net sleeves with bow

Photo credit: courtesy Peter Langner

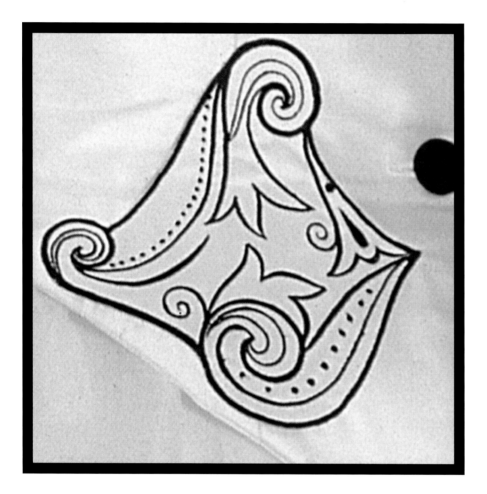

Angelina Baccini
Armadale, Victoria, Australia

Above: Detail of silk pockets

Opposite Page: Renaissance inspired black embroidered collar
and pockets in silk with full organza skirt

Photo credit: courtesy Angelina Baccini

Richard Glasgow, Inc.
New York, New York, USA

Above: Detail of bodice

Opposite Page: Lace halter complements silk twill gown with chapel train

Photo credit: courtesy Richard Glasgow, Inc.

Richard Glasgow, Inc.
New York, New York, USA

Opposite Page:

Above:

Lace bodice complements gossamer silk satin organza gown

Bonaz embroidered cummerbund accents silk satin gown

Photo credit: courtesy Richard Glasgow, Inc.

Richard Glasgow, Inc.
New York, New York, USA

Above: Beaded silk streamers cascade from silk organza strapless gown

Opposite Page: Lace bodice complements silk satin gown with cummerbund

Photo credit: courtesy Richard Glasgow, Inc.

Richard Glasgow, Inc.
New York, New York, USA

Above: Hand-made silk flowers accent silk satin organza gown

Opposite Page: Lace bodice complements silk satin gown with chapel train

Photo credit: courtesy Richard Glasgow, Inc.

Romeo Bastone Couture
Melbourne, Victoria, Australia
1998 Winner Bridal Fashion
Victorian Annual Bridal Industry Awards for Excellence

Above: White de lustred satin gown with guipure lace bodice and hand rouleau
detailing with scattered beading

Photo credit: courtesy Romeo Bastone

Romeo Bastone Couture
Melbourne, Victoria, Australia
1998 Winner Bridal Fashion
Victorian Annual Bridal Industry Awards for Excellence

Above:

Silk ivory and gold brocade gown with matching hat and veil

Photo credit: courtesy Romeo Bastone

Romeo Bastone
Melbourne, Victoria, Australia
1998 Winner Bridal Fashion
Victorian Annual Bridal Industry Awards for Excellence

Above: A timeless glamourous gown of lemon de lustred satin with halterneck bodice and organza overlay skirt

Opposite Page: Glamorous ivory silk sheath with silk ivory/gold brocade detachable train

Photo credit: courtesy Romeo Bastone

Shane McConnell
Camberwell, Victoria, Australia

Above: Hand-knitted silk bodice with cream and pink shot Thai silk skirt

Opposite Page: Hand-painted bodice and hemline, duchess silk gown with organza underskirt

Photo credit: courtesy Shane McConnell

Above and Opposite:

Shane McConnell
Camberwell, Victoria, Australia

Ivory princess silk satin gown with French guipure
lace bodice and knife-pleated skirt

Photo credit: courtesy Shane McConnell

Shane McConnell
Camberwell, Victoria, Australia

Above and Opposite:

Magnolia Thai silk gown with hand embroidery on bustline and train with brocade upper bodice

Photo credit: courtesy Shane McConnell

Shane McConnell
Camberwell, Victoria, Australia

Above and Opposite:

Deep magnolia-coloured strapless silk gown with black
embroidery and heavy draped skirt

Photo credit: courtesy Shane McConnell

Above and Opposite:

Shane McConnell
Camberwell, Victoria, Australia

Silk faille gown with Italian lace bodice and brooched detailing

Photo credit: courtesy Shane McConnell

Shane McConnell
Camberwell, Victoria, Australia

Ice-blue silk satin two-piece gown with draped bodice
and asymmetrical sleeve

Photo credit: courtesy Shane McConnell

Shane McConnell
Camberwell, Victoria, Australia

De lustred silk satin with angle draped bodice and brocade insert skirt

Photo credit: courtesy Shane McConnell

Shane McConnell
Camberwell, Victoria, Australia

Above:

Strapless gown in duchess satin and bolero over-jacket in textured fabric

Photo credit: courtesy Shane McConnell

Special Days Bridal Wear
West Sussex, United Kingdom

Opposite Page: Two-tone beaded duchess satin gown

Above: Back view of ivory and coffee duchess satin gown

Photo credit: Tim Poulton

Special Days Bridal Wear
West Sussex, United Kingdom

Above: Jacket/bodice/waistcoat in brocade with skirts of silk

Opposite Page: Green brocade bodice/jacket with tan silk skirts

Photo credit: Tim Poulton

Special Days Bridal Wear
West Sussex, United Kingdom

Opposite: Full length ivory beaded gown with gold filigree silk cape

Above: Burgundy silk cape over tulle gown

Photo credit: Tim Poulton

Special Days Bridal Wear
West Sussex, United Kingdom

Above: Gold silk tulle maid's gown with ivory trim

Opposite Page: Ivory and gold silk dupion gown

Photo credit: Tim Poulton

Elina Bridal
by Jane Yeh
Newmarket, Auckland, New Zealand

Above: Detail of pearled cornelli

Opposite Page: Thai silk gown with full bodice featuring pearled cornelli work and softly pleated skirt forming a train

Photo credit: courtesy Lesley Walker/NZ Bride & Groom Magazine; model by Megan Yule Nova Models

Sposa Bella Mfg. Ltd.
Birmingham, United Kingdom

Above: Thea: French crepe gown featuring embroidered panels on bodice, sleeves and train

Opposite Page: Portia: classic shape in heavy duchess satin featuring neck and shoulder line in braid embroidery in ivory with gold/silver thread

Photo credit: Adrian Charles Photography

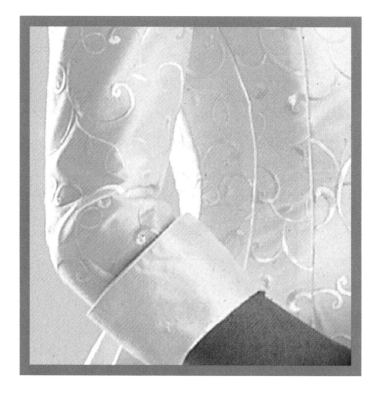

Sposa Bella Mfg. Ltd.
Birmingham, United Kingdom

Above: Details of gown by Sallie Bee

Opposite Page: Gown by Sallie Bee

Photo credit: Adrian Charles Photography

Sposa Bella Mfg. Ltd.
Birmingham, United Kingdom

Above: Beautiful classic style empire-line gown with bodice in rich
French guipure lace and flowing crepe skirt and train

Opposite Page: Guinevere: Gown by Sallie Bee

Photo credit: Adrian Charles Photography

Sposa Bella Mfg. Ltd.
Birmingham, United Kingdom

Opposite Page:

Gown by Sallie Bee

Above:

Gwyneth: multi-panelled bodice and deep pleated skirt with train in rich brocade
with pearl edged leaves trimming shoulders and back waist

Photo credit: Adrian Charles Photography

Sposa Bella Mfg. Ltd.
Birmingham, United Kingdom

Above: Deborah: empire-line with cornelli embroidery on bodice and sleeves

Opposite Page: Clementine: princess-line dress in plain crepe with over bodice in Austrian guipure lace

Photo credit: Adrian Charles Photography

Sposa Bella Mfg. Ltd.
Birmingham, United Kingdom

Above:

Lavinia: pretty, romantic style with rich brocade bodice and pleated poly dupion skirt into train

Photo credit: Adrian Charles Photography

Sposa Bella Mfg. Ltd.
Birmingham, United Kingdom

Above:

Candice: straight style for plus size brides in plain silk dupion featuring ribbon embroidery
on bodice, sleeves and bow

Photo credit: Adrian Charles Photography

Sposa Bella Mfg. Ltd.
Birmingham, United Kingdom

Opposite Page: Celeste: Play suit in embroidered organza worn with calf length circular skirt

Above: Simple but dramatic bodice in French guipure lace and chiffon panelled skirt

Following Page: Gown by Sposa Bella

Photo credit: Adrian Charles Photography

Sposa Bella Mfg. Ltd.
Birmingham, United Kingdom

Above: Macrame lace bodice, straight crepe skirt with chiffon overskirt

Opposite Page: French guipure lace bodice and sleeves with crepe skirt

Photo credit: Adrian Charles Photography

Shane McConnell
Camberwell, Victoria, Australia

Above: Bodice detail

Opposite Page: Pink Thai silk gown with pleated bodice and skirt

Photo credit: courtesy Shane McConnell

Shane McConnell
Camberwell, Victoria, Australia

Above: Detail of under bust pleating with brooch

Opposite Page: Ivory-coloured A-line gown with guipure bodice
and under bust pleating with brooch

Photo credit: courtesy Shane McConnell

Style of South Yarra
South Yarra, Victoria, Australia

Above:

Mauve de lustred satin bustier and skirt beautifully detailed with delicate ice-coloured laces and jewel beads; criss-cross straps in back and lace train insert

Opposite:

Two-piece bustier mauve gown of de lustred silk with bodice covered in selection of guipure laces and crystal jewel beading

Photo credit: Janne Martin Studios

Style of South Yarra
South Yarra, Victoria, Australia

Above: Strapless white de lustred satin and silk tulle gown detailed in ice-pink and green lace beaded flowers with 2" satin ribbon hemline; bustier features rosette in ice-pink

Opposite: Sharp shouldered free hand beading in white de lustred satin with fish tail and slight chapel train

Photo credit: Janne Martin Studios

Style of South Yarra
South Yarra, Victoria, Australia

Above and Opposite:

Strapless two-piece hand-painted gown featuring boned bodice with aubergine piping and silk hand-painted flowers

Photo credit: Janne Martin Studios

Above and Opposite:

Style of South Yarra
South Yarra, Victoria, Australia

White de lustred satin gown adorned with pale blue flower 'squirl' at back and hand-beaded bodice with sheer netting

Photo credit: Janne Martin Studios

Style of South Yarra
South Yarra, Victoria, Australia

Above and Opposite:

Strapless silk wedding gown with detachable sleeves

Photo credit: Janne Martin Studios

Style of South Yarra
South Yarra, Victoria, Australia

Above: Strapless lemon tulle gown with rainbow coloured lace bodice and full skirt hemmed in 2" lemon satin ribbon forming bustle

Opposite: Strapless organza gown with ruching and lightly detailed bodice in guipure lace

Photo credit: Janne Martin Studios

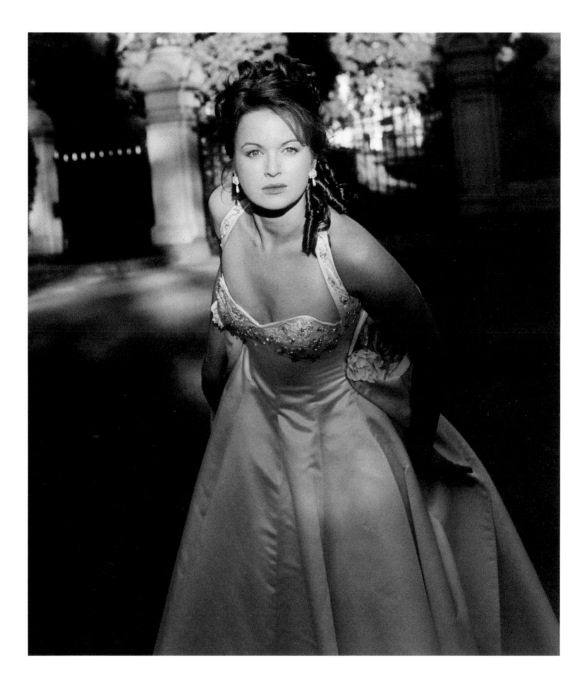

Style of South Yarra
South Yarra, Victoria, Australia

Opposite Page: White de lustred satin princess-line gown hand-beaded in silver rhinestones and crystals

Above: Hand-beaded halter-neck gown of ivory de lustred satin with swirled train of silk gold, cream and apricot flowers

Photo credit: Janne Martin Studios

Style of South Yarra
South Yarra, Victoria, Australia

Above: De lustred champagne satin sheath with free hand-beading, shoestring straps and slight chapel train

Opposite Page: White empress silk corset gown boned with satin ribbons and silk flowers around neckline

Photo credit: Janne Martin Studios

Style of South Yarra
South Yarra, Victoria, Australia

Above:

Empress silk strapless white and royal gown with boned corset and pleated bra cup featuring royal blue silk rosettes and ties leading to a pleated train

Photo credit: Janne Martin Studios

Style of South Yarra
South Yarra, Victoria, Australia

Above:

Strapless ice-blue gown with rough front bodice on full skirt with train; bustle in the back detailed with sky-blue bows

Photo credit: Janne Martin Studios

Style of South Yarra
South Yarra, Victoria, Australia

Ungara brocade with crystal at front bodice neckline, piping
at neckline in sage velvet with matching fitted sculptured jacket

Photo credit: Janne Martin Studios

Style of South Yarra
South Yarra, Victoria, Australia

Above: Medieval style gown in cream and gold silk with bodice piped in gold and silk braid detailing on neckline and skirt edge

Opposite Page: White ungaro brocade beautifully piped in velvet cording, sculptured neckline and shoestring straps

Photo credit: Janne Martin Studios

Opposite and Above:

Kiss Bridal Design Ltd
Stow on the Wold, Gloucestershire, United Kingdom

Gowns by Kiss Bridal Design Ltd

Photo credit: courtesy Kiss Bridal Design Ltd

Kiss Bridal Design Ltd
Stow on the Wold, Gloucestershire, United Kingdom

Above and Opposite:

Gowns by Kiss Bridal Design Ltd

Photo credit: courtesy Kiss Bridal Design Ltd

Elina Bridal
by Jane Yeh
Newmarket, Auckland, New Zealand

Above Left: Elegant sheath gown in French embroidered tulle featuring detachable train

Photo credit: Lesley Walker/courtesy NZ Bride & Groom Magazine; model by Clynne Model Management

Bellantuono Diffusione srl
Milan, Italy

Above Right: Beaded bodice complements soft gown with lace bustle

Photo credit: courtesy Bellantuono

Connie Simonetti
Armadale, Victoria, Australia

Opposite Page: Pure silk satin gown featuring bustier style bodice and Victorian drape on skirt

Photo credit: Sylvanna Spagnuolo

HEADWEAR & JEWELLERY

Wendy Louise Designs
Surry Hills, NSW, Australia

Above Left: Silver and diamante floral

Above Right: Medieval crown ruby crystals

Opposite Page: Scattered pearls in soft gold setting

Photo credit: courtesy Wendy Louise Designs

Wendy Louise Designs
Surry Hills, NSW, Australia

Above: Fine seed pearl detail

Opposite Page: Hand-coloured roses

Photo credit: courtesy Wendy Louise Designs

Wendy Louise Designs
Surry Hills, NSW, Australia

Above: Roses, pearls and tiny forget-me-nots

Opposite Page: Roses amidst leaves and tendrils

Photo credit: courtesy Wendy Louise Designs

Wendy Louise Designs
Surry Hills, NSW, Australia

Above : Antique 'blush' crystals

Photo credit: courtesy Wendy Louise Designs

Wendy Louise Designs
Surry Hills, NSW, Australia

Above:

Delicate pearl and diamante

Photo credit: courtesy Wendy Louise Designs

Wendy Louise Designs
Surry Hills, NSW, Australia

Opposite Page: Swarovski crystal set in silver

Above: Bold golden roses

Photo credit: courtesy Wendy Louise Designs

Wendy Louise Designs
Surry Hills, NSW, Australia

Above:

Daisies in a field of clover

Photo credit: courtesy Wendy Louise Designs

Wendy Louise Designs
Surry Hills, NSW, Australia

Above: Ice-blue vintage glass and crystals

Photo credit: courtesy Wendy Louise Designs

Leanne Michaels
Hyde Park, SA, Australia

Pennino Story; elegant diamond design headpiece and coordinating accessories

Opposite Page: Pennino Necklace; satin silver with fine pearls

Photo credit: Tim Williams Photography

Leanne Michaels
Hyde Park, SA, Australia

Opposite Page: Marcasite Tiara; antique silver, crystal and soft grey pearl

Above: Marcasite Choker and Earrings; antique silver, crystal and grey pearl

Photo credit: Tim Williams Photography

Stephanies
East Malvern, Victoria, Australia

Above: I Dream: tiara heavily encrusted with Swarovski light sapphire crystals, pearls and diamantes

Opposite Page: Castles: ballerina-style crown of delicate filigree mixed with jewels

Photo credit: Mauro Pomponio

Stephanies
East Malvern, Victoria, Australia

Above: Gwenivieve: sterling silver vintage tiara set with garnets and marcasite

Opposite Page: Faberge: designed for the March 1998 Bridal Fashion Week theme of Faberge show 'Independent Visions'

Photo credit: Mauro Pomponio

Crowns of Splendour
Reservoir, Victoria, Australia

Above: Headwear and jewellery by Sharon Vikentios

Photo credit: Ardmillan Studio

Stephanies
East Malvern, Victoria, Australia

Opposite Page: Windsor: designed by request for a royal English tiara

Photo credit: Mauro Pomponio

Stephanies
East Malvern, Victoria, Australia

Above Left: Crystal Castles: filigree tiara encrusted with teardrop crystals, crystals and pearls

Above Right: Eva: gold filigree work meets with crystal and diamante jewels

Opposite Page: Whitney Rose: hand-made, painted porcelain roses suspended amid crystals
and a variety of pearls highlight this 'delicate' tiara

Photo credit: Mauro Pomponio

Stephanies
East Malvern, Victoria, Australia

Above: Severine: golden crown of fine hand-made porcelain flowers and leaves combine with antique pearls from the 20s & 30s

Opposite Page: Lou Lou: modern tiara in silver delicately completed with Swarovski crystals

Photo credit: Mauro Pomponio

Above and Opposite:

Crowns of Splendor
Reservoir, Victoria, Australia

Headwear and jewellery by Sharon Vikentios

Photo credit: Ardmillan Studio

Crowns of Splendor
Reservoir, Victoria, Australia

Above and Opposite:

Headwear and jewellery by Sharon Vikentios

Photo credit: Ardmillan Studio

Crowns of Splendor
Reservoir, Victoria, Australia

Opposite Page:

Headwear and jewellery by Sharon Vikentios

Photo credit: Ardmillan Studio

Wilde Things Original Designs
Balwyn, Victoria, Australia

Above Left: Lou-Lou

Above Centre: Chloe

Above Right: Laurel

Photo credit: Ross Sanfilippo/Fineline

Wilde Things Original Designs
Balwyn, Victoria, Australia

Eden

Photo credit: Ross Sanfilippo/Fineline

Jeanette Maree
Elsternwick, Victoria, Australia

Above :

Bridal sets: classical in design, combining pearls
and Swarovski crystals set in 23ct gold-plate pieces

Photo credit: courtesy Jeanette Barnes

Jeanette Maree
Elsternwick, Victoria, Australia

Above :

Bridal sets: capturing colours reflected from flowers
or bridesmaids' gowns into your own jewellery, creates
an individual look

Photo credit: courtesy Jeanette Barnes

Opposite Page and Above:

Jeanette Maree
Elsternwick, Victoria, Australia

Bridal Jewellery: simple jewellery to complement
or something more detailed to make a statement,
roses are always a popular choice

Photo credit: courtesy Jeanette Barnes

Above and Opposite Page:

Jeanette Maree
Elsternwick, Victoria, Australia

Bridesmaids' Jewellery: bridesmaids play a large role in the memories of the wedding day; in keeping with the bride or dressed in their own colour themes, jewellery and hair accessories complete the picture

Photo credit: courtesy Jeanette Barnes

Kathy Davidson Designs
Malvern, Victoria, Australia

Above Top: Rose band with dark leaf

Above Bottom: Rose band, autumn gold tones

Photo credit: David Meldrum courtesy Kathy Davidson Designs

Kathy Davidson Designs
Malvern, Victoria, Australia

Above Top: | Rose and lily band, pearl finish

Above Bottom: | Arum lily comb, parchment tint

Photo credit: David Meldrum courtesy Kathy Davidson Designs

Kathy Davidson Designs
Malvern, Victoria, Australia

Above: Large rose and rosebud comb

Photo credit: David Meldrum courtesy Kathy Davidson Designs

Kathy Davidson Designs
Malvern, Victoria, Australia

Above:

Floral circlet, pearl finish

Photo credit: David Meldrum courtesy Kathy Davidson Designs

Kathy Davidson Designs
Malvern, Victoria, Australia

Above: Victorian style wax flower headpiece

Opposite Left: Blossom and bud band

Opposite Right Top: Floral orange blossom garland

Opposite Right Bottom: 1940s style wax floral head piece

Photo credit: David Meldrum courtesy Kathy Davidson Designs

Candy Spender Jewels
Prahran East, Victoria, Australia

Above: Light topaz slink choker, 22ct gold-plated pewter with Swarovski crystals

Photo credit: Candy Spender Jewels

Candy Spender Jewels
Prahran East, Victoria, Australia

Above:

Indian chain-mail, 22ct gold-plated pewter with Swarovski crystals

Photo credit: Candy Spender Jewels

Candy Spender Jewels
Prahran East, Victoria, Australia

Opposite Page:

Multi-stranded Japanese costume pearls with large Swarovski crystal

Photo credit: Philip Castle courtesy Candy Spender Jewels

Helena Platanic
Northcote, Victoria, Australia

Above:

Mermaid: turquoise encrusted pewter neckpiece

Photo credit: courtesy Helena Platanic Design

Helena Platanic
Northcote, Victoria, Australia

Above:

Storm: exquisite diamante necklace encased in gold

Photo credit: courtesy Helena Platanic Design

Helena Platanic
Northcote, Victoria, Australia

Above: Charms & Trinkets: gift charms magnificently jewelled with
crystals and moonstones

Photo credit: courtesy Helena Platanic Design

Helena Platanic
Northcote, Victoria, Australia

Above:

Chamonix: diamante encrusted marcasite tiara with
matching double-tiered neckpiece

Photo credit: courtesy Helena Platanic Design

Helena Platanic
Northcote, Victoria, Australia

Above:

Crowned couture

Photo credit: courtesy Helena Platanic Design

Helena Platanic
Northcote, Victoria, Australia

Sincerity: light amethyst necklet/choker

Photo credit: courtesy Helena Platanic Design

Helena Platanic
Northcote, Victoria, Australia

Royal cameo

Photo credit: courtesy Helena Platanic Design

Helena Platanic
Northcote, Victoria, Australia

Above: Romany: amethyst and pale ruby crystal neckpieces with matching crown

Photo credit: courtesy Helena Platanic Design

Above:

Helena Platanic
Northcote, Victoria, Australia

Azuria: midnight Austrian crystal choker and necklet

Photo credit: courtesy Helena Platanic Design

Crowns of Splendor
Reservoir, Victoria, Australia

Above: Headwear and jewellery by Sharon Vikentios

Photo credit: Ardmillan Studio

Crowns of Splendor
Reservoir, Victoria, Australia

Headwear and jewellery by Sharon Vikentios

Photo credit: Ardmillan Studio

Le Diademe
Mulgrave, Victoria, Australia

Above: Set of tiara, necklace and earrings and matching brooch;
topaz stones and crystals

Photo credit: Terry Phelan

Le Diademe
Mulgrave, Victoria, Australia

Above: Necklace and earrings in pearls and crystals

Photo credit: Terry Phelan

Le Diademe
Mulgrave, Victoria, Australia

Above:

Set of tiara, necklace and earrings in pale blue pearls, stones and crystals

Photo credit: Terry Phelan

Le Diademe
Mulgrave, Victoria, Australia

Above: Tiara with pale blue stones, pearls and crystals

Photo credit: Terry Phelan

Le Diademe
Mulgrave, Victoria, Australia

Above:

Choker of pearls and crystals; matching tiara

Photo credit: Terry Phelan

Le Diademe
Mulgrave, Victoria, Australia

Above:

Set of tiara, earrings and necklace in pearls and old gold beads

Photo credit: Terry Phelan

Le Diademe
Mulgrave, Victoria, Australia

Above: Intricate band of pearls, crystals and diamantes with matching earrings

Opposite Page: Necklace and earrings in diamantes and crystals

Photo credit: Terry Phelan

INDEX

ACKNOWLEDGMENTS

We wish to thank all participating firms for their valuable contribution to the publication and especially the following firms who provided photographs for the following pages:

Page 6, Contents
Mika Inatome
Photo credit: courtesy Mika Inatome

Page 8, Wedding Dresses Divider
Mika Inatome
Photo credit: courtesy Mika Inatome

Page 142, Headwear & Jewellery Divider
Stephanies
Photo credit: Mauro Pomponio

Page 214, Index
Helena Platanic
Photo credit: courtesy Helena Platanic Designs